Many of us go through life never identifying how our greatest trials are connected to our greatest struggles. Joe does a great job connecting the extreme trials he experienced to the sexual bondage that hindered him for decades. Through reading vulnerable stories and gaining a rich understanding of intimacy with Christ, you will be inspired to experience the freedom that you can have in your soul by identifying and dealing with the traumas of your past. I highly recommend *Putting Out the Fire!*

Matt Cline
Restored Ministries
www.restoredministries.ca

Putting Out the FIRE

*A personal journey from bondage
to sexual freedom*

JOE WALKER

WESTBOW
PRESS®
A DIVISION OF THOMAS NELSON
& ZONDERVAN

WestBow Press books may be ordered through booksellers or by contacting:

WestBow Press
A Division of Thomas Nelson & Zondervan
1663 Liberty Drive
Bloomington, IN 47403
www.westbowpress.com
844-714-3454

ISBN: 978-1-6642-6680-3 (sc)
ISBN: 978-1-6642-6682-7 (hc)
ISBN: 978-1-6642-6681-0 (e)

Library of Congress Control Number: 2022909214

Print information available on the last page.

WestBow Press rev. date: 07/25/2022

CONTENTS

INTRODUCTION

This story is about my exposure to pornography and its effects on me as a teen and as an adult. It is also about certain personal experiences that changed my life forever.

The purpose for authoring this book is to help all those struggling with porn addiction. My heart goes out to Christian men who love God but have guilt regarding sexual impurity and who struggle against giving in to compromise. When reading my story, you may see some similarities in background experiences. One of my experiences is exceptional, and I doubt that many have suffered the physical injury that was unique to my own background.

The difference in a successful campaign against pornography will be the actions you took or still need to take. The examples in this book are to inform you about the seriousness of this addiction and the help that is out there.

We are unique individuals, and how each individual becomes involved with porn will vary. The responses to that involvement, and the actions needed, will determine whether we have a successful outcome.

What you will read is the way I became addicted and the steps I took to extract myself from my addiction.

This will be a blunt and descriptive telling of my story. I will share with you the struggles I encountered and how these impacted my view of the world around me.

The steps I took to overcome were difficult but necessary. I never would have succeeded if I had kept this habit hidden. I had to get help or stay the same. That was not an option for me. I suffered from personal trauma; I suffered shame and I suffered rejection. I overcame my addiction and so can you.

1

THE PRISON THAT
WAS MY HOME

THE FAMILY OF MY PAST

I grew up in a French community, and we were the only English family on the block. There was a German family on the other street, but we were it for English families. The French were somewhat tolerant of having an English family in their neighborhood. I've had my ups and downs with them. In my early teens, the Front de la libération du Québec (FLQ) became prominent, and some French folk, with their ideology, just wanted to fight the English.

English and French families were in one another's crosshairs. Local gangs existed in both the French and English communities and were sometimes just one mile apart. We beat up on each other from time to time, but the situation eventually deescalated so that we didn't have to keep looking over our shoulders.

I had it rough, and often became the target of discrimination and bullying from both sides of the divide. The English boys did not like that I had an English last name but a heavy French accent, and the French did not like that there was an English boy in their French school. It was difficult to have friends in that environment.

But what I'm about to share is a whole different story of my youth. The difficulties I had with the biases and dislikes because of language or culture pale in comparison to the sexual content of this story.

In addition to this community hardship, my own family also suffered from poor communication and limited social skills, which affected the way we interacted as a family. In retrospect, I now see my family as somewhat dysfunctional. This was an internal difficulty that I had to contend with as well. I did not know this until years later when I saw what normal was.

My father liked his beer and liquor. When he was angry, it usually was because he had been drinking. Otherwise, he was decent enough. He often kept to himself. Our family seemed to be a burden at times for him. I understand that there are struggles to raising a family, so I appreciate that he spent many of our growing-up years working out of province on Northern Canada projects.

I once said that if all there was to life was what I had experienced by the age of twenty, then I'd rather not live. I was starting to ask profound questions, such as, "Why am I here" and "Is there really a

God?" When you get to that point in your life, you reach a serious mindset. For me, the answers, in one form or another, had to be forthcoming. There were no two ways about it.

I already cautioned you that some of the details of my life were agonizing and may be difficult to read. They were difficult to live through. I will attempt to be objective about what I write in order to present an accurate picture of how things were and how I found my way out of the horrible pit I had created for myself. I lived in a prison of fear and isolation, and this was the ultimate prison sentence I imposed on myself. I have left out other personal background information to respect the privacy of others.

A BAD ACQUAINTANCE

I was first exposed to pornography when I was nine years old. While bored one day, I wandered into my parents' room and started exploring. My dad was at work, and my mother was out doing some errands for our family. I found a collection of pornography that my father kept in his dresser drawer. When I discovered those pornographic images, they seemed to leap out at me. I was confused about what I saw. I did not know what I was looking at. I had no filters or defense mechanisms to enable me to understand the images or prevent them from attaching to my inner self.

It felt the way candy feels on the taste buds. There was a certain fascination and perplexity with which I viewed these photos. The images were doing something to me, and I was not even aware of it. My brain chemistry was changing. This played out later in life as I developed an addiction to viewing those images.

I would look at my dad's porn whenever I had a chance. The kicker is that I did not even know why I found it interesting, maybe even appealing. This lasted for about a year until, one day, the porn was gone. It just vanished, and there was no porn to be found. I suspected my father knew I was going through his sock drawers and finding his stash of porn. He had frowned at me a few times in those early days, but he had never talked to me about it. Little did I know what that early exposure had done to me. Those first images are still with me today.

A FEW YEARS LATER

In my growing-up years, I mostly stayed out of my father's way. He spent years working out of town, and I think that suited both of us fine. I hung around with a slightly older friend of the family. My mother was glad for the companionship I was enjoying for a time, as my father spent much time working in the north of Canada.

At first, we played some fun games. Then the

games turned into the kind of things that some would not find very funny. We would stomp on small ketchup packages and watch the spray hit the shoes or pants of people in crowded streets. We rang multiple doorbells all at once in a large apartment building and bought stink bombs for elevators. You get the picture. We were foolish in our actions.

One day, while we were goofing off at my house, this friend approached me with the idea of masturbating. I had not done so prior, and I had no idea what he was talking about. He showed me by masturbating me to an orgasm. The action later had a bad consequence for me. The experience was both ecstatic and shocking. Also, my attitude changed quickly, as I realized that this experience should have been reserved for marriage. Don't ask me how I knew this, but I just knew. I felt taken advantage of. This was my first sexual experience. Afterward, my friend and I no longer hung out. It was my choice not to. My mother knew something had happened, but I did not talk about it. However, I was hooked on the feeling the experience gave me.

After I discovered sex, I began to indulge in masturbation. This gave me a false sense of well-being. My memory of the images from a few years prior fueled my lust, and masturbation became a nasty habit of self-medicating. It is an understatement to say that it surpassed most other pleasures. My propensity to act out in this way seemed insatiable. It was a convenient way to escape from the pain of loneliness. Pornography was not as readily available in those days as it is today. I used my imagination a lot.

One day, at the age of fourteen, with the door closed, I was masturbating in my bedroom. As I was reaching climax, I heard my father's footsteps walking down the hallway toward my bedroom. In a moment of fear and panic, I suddenly pushed down on my penis to avoid being caught in the act. This action caused a sharp pain in my sex organ, but the swelling quickly went away. I had torn some sort of muscle. It turned out that my father simply walked past to use the washroom. I groaned at the realization of what had just happened.

Years later, in my early forties, a physician told me I had torn a supporting ligament and developed curvature in my organ. I could have had it repaired earlier on, but how was I to discuss this incident with my parents at the time? I was too ashamed to speak of it for I would have to explain why I had been masturbating in the first place. Again, I bottled in my feelings. That was a mistake.

The healthy relations between fathers and children are vital to a safe and secure family. The consequences of dysfunction, and lack of open and honest communication are much more pronounced than one can imagine. No wonder teens or young people consider suicide as the only solution to many of their experienced pains. I was eventually headed in that direction.

After the injury, I began to obsess and fret about what had happened. It is very difficult to explain what I felt as a distinction between myself and other boys. I hung out with the guys who did drugs and drank lots of beer. It was the cool thing to do, and I needed to fit in somewhere. I did some drugs and drank beer because this helped dull the deep psychological pain I felt about being different. This was my secret condition, my secret place, my secret pain.

I will focus on how I not only survived but how I became successful. My goal is to have victory in every area.

Free to travel but stuck within my own limitations

Over time, I developed two versions of myself. One acted out and carried on with friends to keep up the appearance of being one of the gang. The other receded into a shell on the inside. I spent lots of time alone reading comics, *Hot Rod* magazines, and satire magazines. I also went for long walks alone that helped me ponder many things about myself. I dreamed of what normal boys often did with girls as my teenage world passed me by. I, on the other hand, avoided potentially embarrassing situations.

My concept of normal relationships between men and women was warped by porn. I lived in both worlds that I had created for myself simultaneously. My social skills suffered, and I had few friends that I hung out with. I was in hiding.

The greatest fear I had was the possibility of failing to please a young lady sexually. What if she noticed the bend in my penis? What if I could not get an erection when it counted the most? For teenage boys, that can be a big part of existing. Just the thought of the possibility of being laughed at or rejected by a girl was more than I could bear. Worse would be knowing that my condition was talked about in the gossip circles. I did not want to take that risk. This feeling of fear and alienation increased as I grew older. To me this was a disaster waiting to happen. Besides this fear, there was always a pain associated at the weak point of the penis whenever there was pressure applied.

This fear of potential failure took its toll, and I quickly realized that I was truly miserable inside. All this, combined with a sex addiction, pushed me to an edge that was dangerous.

CONSEQUENCES

One sunny morning after a night of rain, I watched my father, my uncle, and some neighbors trying to free our moving truck from where it was stuck in the mud. There was a lot of grunting and pushing, revving of the engine, and mud flying everywhere. The tires smoked as they heated up the wet clay, but they remained in their ruts. It took a little while to get the truck free, but not without some cursing and a slick burn of tires on the lawn that went for almost ten feet. The rocking back and forth was most amusing. I found the sight most entertaining as grown men fought furiously to dislodge the vehicle.

I asked myself some questions about what I had observed. Were the tires bald? Did my father back the truck into a slippery area of the property without knowing that it was wet? It had rained the previous evening and it was muddy for sure.

I envisioned how the scenario played out as I observed it. The point I came to was that there were some bad decisions made. When we make wrong choices, the consequences sometimes come with unforeseen penalties, and somebody always pays the price. That is the fact in life for everyone living on this planet. Bad choices lead to bad results, and bad results lead to pain.

The sad part of consequences is that others often suffer for one person's mistakes and misdeeds. My father used to say, "Life is what you make it." But in those early teenage years, it was more about how my father made life for our family.

By the time I finished high school, my mother was after me to continue my education. First, I needed three credits in a high school English class that I had failed.

I enrolled in continuing education in the city of Montreal, taking a night course to get those credits. Unbeknownst to me, I found out I registered for the wrong English class. I wanted to cry because the class I needed to be in was full.

My mother encouraged me to attend a local college. I turned her down. Too risky was my thought, because it would be full of boys and girls. My imagination kept me from going in that direction.

The other option presented to me was attending a local trade and technical school. That was my only option for school if I wanted to keep living at home. The other option was to get a job. I chose the tech school as my mom offered to pay the six-month course. I studied auto and diesel mechanics. I was seventeen when I enrolled.

It was at this trade school that a classmate befriended me. We would leave early from class and drink down pints of beer. We hung around the city parks, alleys, and wherever we could waste time. But he took advantage of my friendship. He invited me to his house one day, and we ate homemade soup that he prepared. I was famished, so I ate with zest that bowl of soup. I looked up at my friend and he was grinning at me. I soon became drowsy and passed out at the table. The soup was laced with sedatives. I woke up the next day in his apartment, just before noon, to find myself on a fold-out couch with my pants undone. He was not around, so I left right away. I cannot tell you if anything happened, but I did not see him anymore and trade school had finished.

By the age of twenty, I could no longer bear what had become of my life. My health was deteriorating. I also had the nasty habit of masturbation as my drug of choice to ease the burden that my life had become.

In retrospect, angry and alcoholic fathers do not make for secure, comfortable home environments. I had always blamed my father for the bad things that happened in our family and, to be sure, he was certainly guilty for his share. But to be fair, not everything was his fault. However, things such as emotional abuse, alcohol, anger, and physical and sexual abuse were in the mix of ingredients in my family background. Now you get the picture because, in retrospect, I viewed our family as dysfunctional. I was ashamed of our family, and I was ashamed of myself for not being able to have prevented some of those events.

If help would have been available then as it is today, I would have recovered from past wounds much sooner.

I had experienced enough of this stuff; I started to bail out of life. My thinking was deteriorating, and I became angrier over the course of time. I saw things as worse than they were. I found myself withdrawing early in life into my own little world. I would spend as much time as possible reading comic books or going for long walks to pass the time. My reclusiveness grew over time because of fear of exposure, and this led to some bad habits and attitudes. I did not develop any long-lasting relationships prior to the age of twenty,

Fear is a paralysing emotion. As stated in 2 Tim 2:7, "For God has not given us a spirit of fear, but of power and of love and of a sound mind." There are many types of fear, and everyone experiences fear at one time or another in their lives.

In early spring of 1973, I decided to move away from home. I moved 300 miles away to Ottawa. I rented a room in an old house with an acquaintance who was heavily into drugs. The move was an act of desperation. I needed to get away, to be by myself to reflect on my life and what it had become. I ate less often and was losing weight.

At this juncture, I decided to take a step of faith. I asked God if He really existed. In a letter I wrote to Him, I described my desperation and the deep hole I found myself in. I placed the letter in a Bible that my mother had given me, in hopes that He might see it there.

A NEW BEGINNING

Three months after moving to Ottawa, my outlook got desperate. I realized that I carried my skeletons with me. I could not pretend otherwise; depression was setting in a little more, and my drive to go on living was waning. I was in the world, but without hope and hopelessly lost.

I convinced myself that death would probably be better than the prison I built for myself. I was trapped in *fear* and did not see a way out. I could not visualize having any kind of future that didn't include pain, exposure, and loss—a future with no intimate relationships, no friends, and no hope.

I had reached that point. My desperation drove me to ask myself some questions. *Why was I born anyway? And what is the purpose of life? Is there a God, and does he care?* Even though I experienced God, or what I thought was God, at certain times in my life, I still did not know who He was or if it was even possible to have a personal connection with Him. I decided that if there was no God, there would be no point in living any longer. My state of mind was depressing. However, the fear of death, its permanence, and its finality, served to set my focus in at least one last place of inquiry.

You would have to climb into my mind to really understand how utterly hopeless I felt. To have a long and fulfilling life with a lifelong spouse, as most guys dream about, seemed utterly impossible to visualize.

As I mentioned, once you ask the question "Is there a God?" the answer must present itself to you so you can decide whether you continue to hope or give up living. Too many people give up hope, I believe, just when there might be an answer that they somehow failed to see. When you are depressed, the light at the end of the tunnel just gets dimmer. Of course, when you're in your right mind, you can see the options. When you are in a depressive state, you can no longer reason or see the bright side. I speak from experience. If you are in that state, please tell somebody, see your doctor, or check yourself in to a medical facility.

Those few months I lived in Ottawa became for me the do or die life. I soon realized that I needed to reach out to a higher power, and not one second later, I prayed: God, are you real? I've made a mess of my life and you're my last hope. If you are real, please reveal yourself to me, I really need to know. Otherwise, I do not want to go on living like this anymore.

This prayer I wrote out one day in my shabby rental. I then took the note paper and thought, *Where can I put this so that God can see it?* Bless my mom; she had given me a little Bible to take with me while alone in Ottawa. I figured if there was any place where God was going to see it, it was in the Bible. I folded the note in half and placed it in the center of the Bible, thinking that if God was real, he would see the note in there.

During those days in Ottawa, I walked the streets and parks in serious contemplation. I was observing the same routines that I saw the days before. But I now was looking for something that would confirm God's existence. On a side note, when you pray to God for help in your own situation, look for indications in your surroundings that He's going to answer your prayers.

One day, a young man stopped me as I was walking, and asked if I'd be interested in hearing how the organization he was involved with helped him.

I answered him, "Sure, why not." We walked half a block to an entrance with The Science Church written on the front. I noted to myself that there must be scientists involved with this church. Surely, they might have an answer for me.

I followed him to the second-floor office, and he sat behind the desk and seemed excited to have me there. He told me all the stuff this group did for him and the job it provided. He presented me with a form to fill out, and said that someone would assess it and call me for an appointment. I sat down feeling a little hopeful.

As I picked up the pen and was just about to write in the first space, the young man spoke and said, "One of the main things you'll learn is that we don't believe in God." He said this as a matter of pride. He continued, "In a matter of time, you'll learn that the answers are in you." When he said that I would come to realize this and adopt their belief system, I stopped writing. I was stunned by the boldness of his statement that he did not believe in God.

It was a strange thing to feel resentment and to object to his disbelief in God. I had no real proof that God existed but leaned on the side of caution. It was at that point that I immediately decided this was not for me. I told him so and said that I believed in God.

I had discovered a kind of faith that helped me speak my mind. I doubted at this point that he could help me any further. I left right away and could not get out of that place fast enough.

On another occasion, a young lady talked to me as I strolled one Sunday afternoon near the Parliament grounds. She was very friendly and wanted me to meet some of the people who helped her and many others find their way. I was enchanted and was prepared to follow her to their site.

She began to speak badly about the people around who did not give her the time of day. I was surprised by her attitude, because she said that she was a Christian. I knew that Christians were kind, charitable, and friendly. I thought that one should not speak badly about people if one is a Christian. This gave me pause for thought. I sensed that this was not going to turn out well. I came up with an excuse and left her standing there. I could see that she was quite disappointed and put off.

Years later, I learned that this group was another religious offshoot run by a cultist organization. Their mode was to have young ladies recruit men and bring them back to their compound. Then they would have sex with them and keep the recruits there so that the organization could begin brainwashing them in their brand of religion. In retrospect, I'm glad I listened to that warning sensation and pulled out. I was like a bird that escaped from the fowler's snare.

On a beautiful summer day, one of Ottawa's best days, the streets were turned into a market that spanned several blocks. One day as I walked down the street, I heard some music that seemed different, a different tune of sorts. As I approached, I noticed a bandstand with musicians and singers. I listened to the end of a song, and a young man spoke up and thanked everyone for coming out. He talked about the purpose of their presence, and said that several of them would fan out into the crowd to answer any questions we might have about the Christian faith. Then they left the stage and went into the crowd. It dawned on me what was happening. I turned away to leave the area. I was hoping to avoid a religious discussion.

As I turned to walk in the other direction, a couple of young Christians were right there in front of me. They introduced themselves and, before I had a chance to assess why they were smiling at me, I was challenged to listen to God's plan for me. Since the two were beautiful young ladies, this helped me to pause a moment.

When they mentioned the name Jesus, my first thought was to say, "Hey, I am a Catholic and I know all I want to know about Jesus." Well, if God could read thoughts, He had just read mine.

He said to me, "Sit down, keep quiet, and listen. You are going to hear something you have never heard before."

Having been told clearly, I said yes to them. We

noticed a couple of benches and so we sat down on them. During the next hour, I heard about God's plan of salvation for my life. They explained the gospel (also known as the Good News) using a booklet called *The Four Spiritual Laws*.[1]

For the first time in my life, I heard something that made perfect sense. There were no yellow lights or internal warning signals like I had felt with the other folk. At the end of our session, and being convinced of what I heard, I accepted what they told me as truth.

I agreed to let them lead me in what is known as the sinner's prayer. I was excited by the possibility of meeting God for the first time in my life. There were some young men nearby, telling me not to listen. They said I should leave, but I ignored them. It astounded me that at this critical juncture, they, who I had never met and did not know, should try to dissuade me from listening to the Truth. The

---

[1] created in 1952 by Bill Bright, founder of Campus Crusade for Christ.

enemy was working overtime. My roommate, who was watching me from a distance, said that he saw demons rolling and thrashing around on the ground.

In retrospect, I can see the demons unhappy to lose a soul to God's Kingdom. I hope they were severely punished for their failure.

Afterward, I went back to my room and sat. I thought seriously about the implications of surrendering my life to Jesus as Lord. There was a cost involved. This was for keeps, I knew. I weighed the trade-off and thought that God was seriously coming up short in the trade-off. But all he wanted was my heart. I accepted God's terms of surrender and I became the net beneficiary.

I just want to mention that I may never have turned to God if I had not suffered from personal trauma. It's within the realm of reason to believe that God used past events in my life to get my attention. And I strongly believe that He used the events but did not cause them. God is not that kind of God, but is a loving, caring, and merciful God who feels and identifies with our pain.

For we do not have a High Priest who cannot sympathize with our weaknesses, but was in all points tempted as we are, yet without sin. Let us therefore come boldly to the throne of grace, that we may obtain mercy and find grace to help in time of need. (Hebrews 4:15–16)

2

PORNOGRAPHY IS A POISONED ARROW

THE ADDICTION CONUNDRUM

I discovered there was a deep well in my soul that porn managed to hide in. My addiction came alive again with the advent of the internet and computers.

This part is dedicated to sufferers of sexual addiction, as it is what I am familiar with. I don't know much about other sorts of addictions, but the principles applied in this book will apply in most cases.

You also will seek to better your response to the *draw*. The draw is this: Yielding to a lust that comes in a moment of weakness to captivate our imaginations with the intent to lead us to commit sin. Lusting is a part of our carnal nature that we received because of the fall in the Garden of Eden.

The more one gives in to lust, the easier it is to commit to acting on it. The opposite is also true. The more one resists the temptation to give in, the stronger the ability to resist. However, in resisting, you cannot rely on your own determination or strength of will. You will fail every time. Dependency on the Lord is the only safe venue to victory.

I used the title above as opposed to The Addiction Mystery since porn addiction is not really a mystery; instead, it is a puzzle of sorts. Does one truly understand the complexity of the human propensity for sexual addictions? It is an enigma, and a most difficult addiction to defeat. I write this because of my own difficulty in finding a lasting solution that was complete and whole. Ultimately, I did find a lasting solution, but for me this took years, and everyone is different. People have different experiences, different backgrounds, and different exposures. A lengthy struggle may not be your case; you may be able to lose the addiction quickly with the right help.

But first let's look at some statistics and descriptions of what scientists have discovered.

*All fires must be put out completely
or they can flare up again*

A person who has problems with sexual fantasies, sexual thinking, or sexual behaviors significantly damages his or her ability to lead a balanced life. Clinical evidence[2] indicate that core functional changes in the brains of people, affected by substance addiction, also appear in the brains of people affected by behavioral addictions. These conditions include gambling, internet surfing, shopping, and sex addiction.

Many who view sexually explicit material often use alcohol or other substances during their most recent sexual encounter. The earlier someone begins using a substance, the more likely it is that he or she will become addicted. Therefore, teens who develop a porn addiction are at a greater risk for developing a substance abuse disorder as well.'

Some of you already know these facts. I want to be honest with you: this beast of an addiction will

---

[2] www.ncbi.nlm.nih.gov/pmc/articles/PMC6352245, Journal List J Clin Med v.8(1); 2019 Jan PMC6352245

probably have to be run through several times. Just when you've thrust it through with the javelin, it raises its ugly head.

Chemical changes occur in the brains of porn addicts as well as other addicts. One's own identity can be affected at a young age. Far-reaching damage from porn can come via images, videos, and the practice and use of various forms of pornography. The younger someone is, the greater the damage.

I was a pre-adolescent boy who found pictures of porn in his father's sock drawer. I had no idea what I was looking at. The images were seared in my brain because I did not filter or categorize what I was seeing. The chemical changes already started to happen as I continued to examine these images over a period of several months. It started the addiction process within me without my even realizing it.

The seeds of those images were sown, and germination took place over the next few years. At age thirteen, I was introduced to masturbation. The pleasure center of my brain was activated when I visualized porn images while masturbating.

GERMINATION AND ROOTS

It is the using of sexually explicit materials which stimulates lust into self-centred acts of masturbation. Porn viewing becomes an obsession. The frequency of viewing porn increases with age. With all the awkward chemical changes that take place in the years between boyhood and adulthood, the child or young person most likely does not understand what is taking place within his or her own soul. The awareness of the pattern of self-medicating gradually becomes apparent as one ages.

There's a real need for education on the dangers of pornographic materials. Unfortunately, many agencies and aid groups have not prioritized the addiction as a worldwide pandemic. But that's a conversation for another time.

If there is abuse or dysfunction in the home, fear and anxieties increase. When things are volatile in the home, the person is driven toward seeking comfort, to acting out (often in anger) or, as is often the case, to self-medicate. He or she begins to find stress relief in various activities that may become addictive. The viewing of explicit materials is a common practice among many young boys and—I hate to mention this—girls as well. This most commonly leads to masturbation to relieve the anxieties or to stimulate the pleasure center. This pattern of behavior is habit forming.

James Dobson, in one of his books[3], says that as juveniles travel the long corridor to adulthood, there are many doors along the way. These doors represent every trap of addiction or belief system that you

---

[3] Preparing for Adolescence: How to Survive the Coming Years of Change Paperback – Dec 15 2005 by Dr. James Dobson (Author)

find along the way in life. When someone opens a door, he or she may find what's inside disgusting, close the door, and never go back. Others may find what is inside that same door appealing. Some characteristic of the person's fallen human nature is hooked by what it experiences, and so the person enters, never to find his or her way out again. For many parents, this is the stuff of nightmares: to see a son or daughter fall into some sort of addiction or lifestyle that is in the process of ruining him or her.

The fantasies, coupled with the pleasurable sensation of masturbation, become the habit that becomes bondage. It also turns into that person's gateway drug of choice: a shelter in the storm of emotional turmoil, probably to be used for years to come. As I mentioned before, addiction also produces chemical changes in the brain so that it becomes easier every time to repeat the same pattern of behaviour. The brain remembers what works. But what may work in the interim may have serious consequences for the future.

This is where the roots of addiction or addictions go deep into the person's sense of self. This behavior follows a pattern that's craftily developed by that individual. It is the addicted self, under the radar of consciousness, which controls the decisions when the true self is at the weakest.

Not everyone follows the pattern of addiction exactly as I've described. We are all individuals and unique in that sense. Our responses to the information we perceive, the exposure, and the practice of the addiction itself will all vary to a certain degree. Finding how porn affects us as individuals is the key.

One of the other reasons for writing this book is to help you find the combination of literature, meetings, group therapy, church, prayer, sponsors, and anything else that helps with the eventual exit plan from the addictions. There must be in your thinking an eventual exit plan from the habits and mindset that addiction to porn produced in you.

How deeply a person is affected depends on several factors. Here are just a few questions I asked myself.

1. Do I have a good self-image?
2. Do I have a good relationship with my parents?
3. Am I an introvert or extravert?
4. Do I experience guilt because I view porn?

These are simple questions that may help to define your position. What I mean by position is any addiction or mindset that is harmful to you. The experiences, the emotions, the thought processes, and the perception of self are all vitally important to determine the depth of the addiction and of the potential damage to the psyche.

TRUTH MATTERS

In retrospect, I asked myself these questions during my past experiences with porn. It was the perfect storm in this regard. The description and questions above are those that applied to me many years ago. I discovered two worlds at war within me. The quest to survive and to understand my life drove me until the day my life changed forever. I had two inner worlds that I lived in one body, and two behaviours in making my way in this world. It's not as disjointed as I make it seem, but disjointed enough to warrant mentioning it.

Now what if I said that I became a Christian at age twenty, that I have been a Christian for forty-five years, and that I struggled with porn occasionally until recently? I know too well the feelings associated with what we may call moral failure. The struggle is between life and death, right and wrong, success and failure. Surrendering to Jesus or doing my own thing is the crucial question! These lie at the intersection of wanting true freedom or continuing in surrender to the physical cravings of sexual addiction. I had a choice.

Before I go on, I wish to extend hope to anyone reading this, especially if you consider yourself a Christian. It is my firm belief that overcoming addiction successfully is ultimately up to the person who wants to overcome his or her addiction to sexual impurities, including porn.

It's important to know that the process of healing is in proportion to how much we are willing to accept the truth about ourselves, and our willingness to consider carefully what the Lord instructs us to do as written in His word. With prayer and guidance from the Holy Spirit, we can act once we recognize that truth. As Jesus said, "And you shall know the truth, and the truth shall make you free" (John 8:32).

This quest for freedom will require times in

prayer, as it did with me. You may not be a Christian, but God loves when people come to Him for help. There are incidents in the Bible where Jesus's disciples were not able to help those who came to them for healing. Even after they were given the authority to do those things, they were not able to perform them. In answer to their question about their lack of success, Jesus said that some things do not work without prayer and/or fasting. As Mark 9:28–29 states, "And when He had come into the house, His disciples asked Him privately, 'Why could we not cast it out?' So He said to them, 'This kind can come out by nothing but prayer and fasting.'" I see porn addiction as that kind of demon. And I believe that Jesus is saying that you need to build up a strong spiritual life in relationship with Him to beat this thing.

Asking God for insight or understanding is what we all should do. This is for all areas of life, from what job to do, what school to attend, and so on.

IT IS ABOUT YOU.

Jonah found himself in the belly of the great fish. One of the things he said while praying was, "Those who regard worthless idols forsake their own Mercy" (Jonah 2:8). He was speaking to himself in remembering that the Lord is much bigger than his present circumstance. I read this passage to mean that to pay attention to secular ideas on sexuality and life in general will lead you to forsake your own mercy (that you have from God). But as I studied the saying "forsake your own mercy," I noticed that one of the interpretations renders it this way: that you'll forsake the kindness and piety you had for God.

In other words, there's the tendency to become calloused or desensitized to God when we ignore the truth about our condition. The same thing happens when we justify our use of porn, even mild porn. The ongoing use of porn results in a diminishing love for God. We'll avoid uncomfortable situations that remind us of our condition. This will keep us away from the very thing we need in our lives. Porn is evil itself in that it does not represent what God had in mind for marriage. Using porn is about satisfying the self. Exposing ourselves to porn or lustful images creates in us lust for the things that lead us away from God, and causes us to be complacent about our own condition.

There is always a good time to examine our thoughts, attitudes, and intentions when about using porn to satisfy a perceived need or want. I was frustrated with my repeated failures that I wanted to quit trying to stop my use of porn. It was like breaching the wall between myself and some disgusting sewer rat. I wanted to compromise and feel good, so I would limit myself to a little bit of porn from time to time. I wanted to let that be where I parked. I became alarmed at my attitude of complacency. I wanted to stop caring, but my conscience said no.

I went to see a counsellor who dealt with sexual issues. He was not very helpful because I did not fall into the pattern of activity that he was convinced I had committed. Most of my fantasies with porn were internal and visual in nature; I did not cross the line into actual practice. Why not, you ask? I remind you that I still lived in my shell and lived in fear of discovery. I'm sure if that was not the case, I would have possibly been among the worst of offenders. But in a way, I was protected from significant sin by my reluctance to act out in real life. In retrospect, my willingness of talking about past personal experiences only came later in life. I could not admit to it on my own. I needed God's help.

The truth is that you and I are addicts if we use porn and cannot stop. The concept that I was an addict was new to me, even though I was thoroughly addicted. I had difficulty accepting the truth. My occasional viewing of porn was a disrespectful act in my relationship to the Lord, not to mention a betrayal to my wife.

This has nothing to do with whether He forgives me or not. It has everything to do with the quality of the relationship I have with Him. It was all about me, my perceptions, my attitudes, and my willingness to act or not.

Did I ever think that I could do this and go on my merry way and pretend that I was fine? God forbid! Therefore, I prayed and fasted on occasion. I needed to get my bearings and realign my purpose and direction, if only to put this matter down once and for all. There were things I put in place that were important. But making my heart right before God is the single most important thing I needed to do.

3

COMPROMISE

Most Christians do not want to continue to be involved with pornography. But the fact is that many Christians are addicted to porn. Some have no idea that they are addicted. Before we realized the brutality of that entire industry, the marketing of distorted sex and its effect on the human soul, it was too late for many of us. But this does not mean we should stay stuck in the rut.

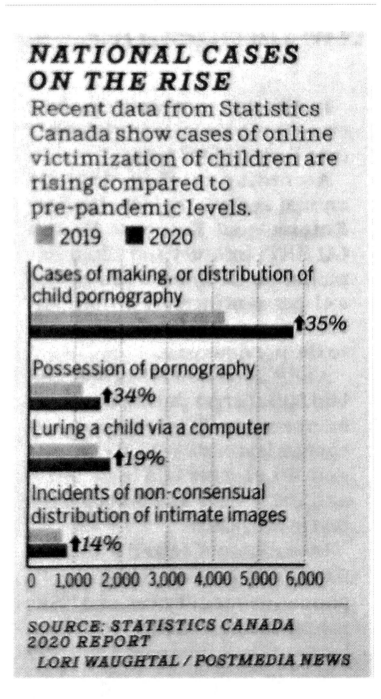

NATIONAL CASES ON THE RISE

Recent data from Statistics Canada show cases of online victimization of children are rising compared to pre-pandemic levels.

2019   2020

Cases of making, or distribution of child pornography
↑35%

Possession of pornography
↑34%

Luring a child via a computer
↑19%

Incidents of non-consensual distribution of intimate images
↑14%

0   1,000 2,000 3,000 4,000 5,000 6,000

SOURCE: STATISTICS CANADA 2020 REPORT
LORI WAUGHTAL / POSTMEDIA NEWS

Another misconception is that addicts can control the intensity or number of times they view porn. That is another lie that we tell ourselves. Or we come up with a detente to make it acceptable to ourselves. It is a twisted sort of justification. We may say that what we are viewing is innocent compared to what is out there. We may see it as an acceptable level because our friends are into it much worse. Those are not the kinds of friends who are helpful when we are serious about changing our behavior and lifestyle!

Others accept a view that is a false teaching in the Christian faith: that the body has little to do with the spiritual aspect of their lives. So what I do in the body does not affect my relationship with God? Nonsense!

Viewing porn also gives men a sense of personal empowerment. This validates the behavior because of the chemicals that flood the human body. The practice of masturbating to various pornographic images contributes to the enforcement and practice of this habit. This habit can lead to the darker side of pornography. (As an example, that the inserted stat demonstrates.) Porn is bad enough, but the descent into child pornography, human abuse, torture, rape, and body mutilation is increasing exponentially. This may not be you, but it can become you. Sin is so deceiving that you can't even see its effect on you.

The addict increasingly needs a higher dose to get the same high he had a year ago or six months ago. It is like developing a tolerance to a certain drug (prescribed or other) so that you no longer get the bang for your buck. Then there's a need for a higher dose. This is a fact, and it applies to the porn addict as well.

But many are deeply convicted. Their addiction is not compatible with the faith they profess. Most have no idea about how to get help, or who to talk to or confide in. Some have given up and thrown in the towel. Many have allowed their use of porn to destroy their marriages, their families, and their faith. Some have even committed suicide over the problem. There is no easy way to say this. We men need to take personal inventory of our lives. We must take a good look at or observe what it is that's driving our repeated use of our drug of choice.

The porn industry has permeated every fabric of society. You cannot go one day without being exposed to some form of it. It's in music, on television, in films, in magazines, and in advertisements, which ensures sex in its many products. YouTube and the internet also have numerous roads to these sites, and in this day, they are mostly free to view.

Think about how your cell phone offers immediate access to the sexual offerings of impurity from any country, in any intensity, and at any time. What is an addicted guy to do to avoid this?

This is a serious issue, particularly for the Christian, and unless it is dealt with, you'll want to keep a low profile. If you are in any kind of Christian ministry, you may wish to step down, albeit temporarily, and get the help you need to overcome the habit. Porn will interrupt the influence of your Christian faith. Its effect on the family will be felt in one way or another. Everything you and I do has a ripple effect that is ongoing in this life. I say this because the statistics are there. I cannot stress enough that many Christians in local churches are addicted to porn.

In his book, *Beneath the Surface: Steering Clear of the Dangers That Could Leave You Shipwrecked*, Bob Reccord talks about his friend Stan, who failed morally. The conversation between Bob and his friend Stan ends with Stan's statement that even though the alarm bells were going off and God's Word was sounding in his life, he chose to ignore them. According to Stan, "I disconnected the wires."[4]

I know exactly what that feels like, being in the

---

[4] Bob Reccord, *Beneath the Surface: Steering Clear of the Dangers That Could Leave You Shipwrecked* (Nashville, TN: B & H Books, 2002, 36.

moment, I've done that very thing. It was like one part of who I was overcame the other part of me that was screaming *no*. But I refused to listen. I was like the three monkeys: one who wouldn't see, one who wouldn't hear, and the other who wouldn't speak out.

Disconnecting the wires is what we do when what we want becomes more important than what God wants. The trickle effect of this scenario starts with a thought that protrudes from our sinful hearts. The idea is a temptation that argues a reasonable, even enticing experience waiting in the wings, and our natures desire that. Our lust bullies us into giving in because we have not learned how to resist it. It seems so much easier to give in sometimes, particularly when we are in pain. We get duller in our sensitivity to God every time we give in.

I remember a time that I was working with my father. He landed a contract to put the rain leaders in the ground and on the roof ceiling. These would catch the rain from the flat roof, funnel it down the vertical stacks, and send it away to the sub-ground piping that led to the city gray water drainage. I was sixteen, or maybe even fifteen, at the time. Back then, contractors used cast iron pipe with hubs and spigots, oakum, and lead to seal the joints together. Oakum is made from a vegetable fiber and is used for packing hub and spigot joints. I had the unenviable job of scooping melted lead with a huge cast iron spoon that weighed a ton empty. You can imagine the weight of that thing when it was full of melted lead.

I had to grab that spoon with two hands, dip, run to the scaffold, and climb to hand the spoon to one of the workers. This sounds easy, but read on. The warehouse roof was in the process of being installed and, in the area where we worked, the roof was not complete. It had rained the night before and the ground was like a minefield. The holes were filled with water, and the ground was uneven and mostly slippery clay. Pieces of old pipe, wood, and cement made it treacherous to traverse. So I spilled some hot lead as I ran slowly to the scaffold. This also came with warnings to be careful from the watchful eyes above.

The guys on the scaffold didn't seem to care about those things. They kept hollering for me to move it, move it, like that song. They smiled as they watched my humble efforts to keep up with the demand. I noted that my father was one of those who smiled as the other two were shouting for me to hurry up.

While this was going on, I also had to feed the melting pot with ingots of lead that melted to liquid. When I first started my job, I noted that there was some gunk at the surface of the melted lead. I asked my dad what it was. He explained that those were the impurities that were a part of the lead ingots. Those impurities were dross that came to the surface as the heat increased to a temperature where the lead melted. Dross is foreign matter, dregs, or mineral waste, in particular, scum formed on the surface of molten metal. He showed me how to remove the dross. He took the large spoon and skimmed the surface of the lead. The dross that accumulated on the spoon was thrown aside. This left behind a shiny lead surface.

The images of that story have remained with me for years. I think of life as one big learning event.

In practicality, our hearts are fill with impurities. When the Lord works on our lives, He sometimes turns up the heat. This has an interesting result. Read on.

Life's events have analogies, paradigms, and metaphors, and one should be willing to learn from these. This is especially true when we find ourselves in the middle of change. I can observe and grow, or go along blindly and stay the same. But that is a misunderstanding of reality, for we do change for better or worse. There is no such thing as staying the same. We are never static. We can benefit from hindsight and maybe, just maybe, avoid repeating the history of our own mistakes.

Let's pretend that the lead ingot is you, the melting pot is your life, and the fire is circumstances, events, incidents, and pretty much everything life throws at you. As natural life happens all around you, you begin to feel the heat. The more difficult or complex life becomes, the more life discloses who you really are. In other words, the real you comes forward. The stress, the fatigue, the anxiety, and anger that heats you up points to something that may be incomplete or unsatisfied in your life. It may well have been this way for quite some time.

In 1995, I discovered porn on the internet. This is when viewing porn became an ongoing habit with me. Many of us developed bad habits to cope with stress. We began to experiment with, among other things, alcohol, smoking, or taking drugs, having sex, gambling, and viewing porn. What is common in this era of self-medication is that the real problem is never dealt with. We've band-aided the pain and carried on, looking forward to the end of the day. That is what happened to me, from 1973 to 1995, I bandaged the addiction till the habit became full blown.

Some people enjoy their bad habits. They will often blame circumstances or other people for the difficulties they experience. They will not look at their own souls or confront their own real selves. They refuse to grow up, and when there is a perception that it's all about them, they reveal their own incompetence and immaturity. The jails are full of people like that. But to be fair, the outside world is also full of self-seekers.

What we really need is for someone to show us how to remove the dross when it shows up in our lives. To what end, you may ask? In the grand scheme of things, it boils down to this: we would become free from our past bad attitudes and habits and become who we were intended to become in the beginning of time before sin led us astray. Flying right is not possible without God.

Early in our marriage, my wife began to suspect that I was struggling with something but was not sure what. I would respond to her that I worked it out, and not to worry. The truth is that I was viewing porn every three to five days. One day, I admitted to her that I was looking at porn. She now knew that this had been true for some time. I reached a place that if I did not get the help I needed, our marriage would disintegrate.

An acquaintance told me about a group called Sexaholics Anonymous, otherwise known as SA. I placed a call and met with a member who vetted me as a candidate. I was approved to attend. I might as well say that my problem was serious enough.

The first meeting was at a church basement. After I went to my first meeting, I knew that this was where I belonged. It took me three more meetings before I could admit that I was an addict.

There is a certain humbling that takes place when you admit you are an addict. It's the surrender of believing that you had control. I did not have control and I quickly realized this as I began to hear the others' stories.

I committed to attending two times a week at two different locations. In retrospect in seems like it was overkill. But for me, I knew this had to be done. I attended these meetings just shy of two years. During that time, my incidents of porn viewing and masturbating decreased. I learned a lot about myself. I began to understand the brokenness that was deep within my soul.

At the end of the two years, I asked the Lord if I could switch to a Christian recovery group called Overcomers Anonymous (OA). He replied that I was in that hospital long enough. I noted that He called it a hospital, which was interesting.

I attended OA for about one and a half years, once a week. This group covered all types of addictions, and used a recovery Bible with lessons and homework. I did work lessons and read various passages of scripture that helped me grow in my understanding.

In the previous group, I worked through the steps of recovery that is like the ten Alcoholics Anonymous steps. I also worked on a testimony that I shared in a group of about twenty-five people, which detailed my entire history, including damaging my penis.

I was praised by the group for my honesty and openness, and I really believe that this was a big help toward my recovery from the addiction. I see now why the Lord gave me the okay to leave that group. I had gone as far as I could within those two years. It was humbling, but it was also helpful toward my full healing.

Reaching the end of a long journey

Four years on, I've come a long way. But I still had

incidents occasionally. For me, I was still torn by the

fact that I still had not fully recovered. I discovered

a book by Timothy Keller on prayer, called, you guessed it, 'Prayer'[5]. I began to pray every second day for twenty to thirty minutes. Over a period of two to three years, I began to pray a little more often.

My failures lessened, and when I failed, I would go in prayer, broken with tears, asking the Lord to help me stop looking at porn. I no longer went to stores and looked at magazines with various photograph of women in lingerie, bikinis, or any kind of suggestive poses. These were not even porn, but they acted as triggers.

I went trigger hunting; I became mindful of anything that would trigger me. Triggers stirred the memories at a time of weakness when lust was fighting me and threatening my sobriety. I even got rid of my television so that I would not channel surf. At the end of several years, I had still compromised

---

[5] Prayer: Experiencing Awe and Intimacy with God by Timothy J. Keller

my values. It would only happen very occasionally, but it was once too many times for me.

A scripture I had read kept going on in my mind. Hebrews warns that today if you hear his voice, do not harden your heart. That word *harden* means to be obstinate or stubborn in the Greek. It's like placing a radio in a floaty, setting it in the water from your boat, and watching it float away. The music is loud, but as it drifts away, the sound diminishes. Soon not only can you not hear it, you can no longer see it.

You get it, right? I find it amazing how quickly a thought, fully armed to the teeth, can get our attention. Why is that, you wonder? It is often a conflict of interest that leads us along the road called downfall. We argue that it's a small matter, a temporary flirtation, a sort of an intriguing dance that is soon over. Yeah, it's over and we've fallen headlong right smack back in that pattern of self-medication. I know this because that is where I was for such a long time. It made me sick to think about my ongoing failures.

I wanted easy solutions to complex problems. One of the problems was that the DJ in my thoughts put in another song, and I would say to myself, *It's just one more dance. It's just one more glass of wine, just one more hour of TV, just one more peek at that magazine.* In his book *AHA*[6], Kyle Idleman states that

> Sin will always take you farther than you wanted to go.

> Sin will always cost you more than what you wanted to pay.

> Sin will always keep you longer than what you wanted to stay.

You cannot control sin. It must be eradicated. I will talk more about that later.

---

[6] AHA: The God Moment That Changes Everything by Kyle Idleman

You've heard the saying "failure through compromise"? Many hear it too late or not at all. How can a fleeting glance lead to such catastrophic moral failure, you ask? It's the difference between a non-addicted person and an addicted one! If the wall has been breached a thousand times, it is no longer a sturdy wall.

According to a traditional understanding of integrity, it is the virtue of holding fast to one's principles in the face of temptations. It is accepted by theorists who write about integrity, that it is incompatible with compromising one's morals.

Author Doug Batchelor writes in his article 'An Amazing Fact'[7]. 'Because of its unusual growth habits, the tropical banyan tree is known as a "strangler fig." These large trees usually start life when their seed is deposited by a bird high in the foliage of another tree. The banyan's roots descend

---

[7] https://www.amazingfacts.org/news-and-features/inside-report/magazine/id/10782/t/compromise--conformity---courage

over the trunk of the host tree, seeking out the soil below. Once they have rooted themselves, the roots of the strangler fig rapidly thicken and lengthen. Where the fig roots cross each other, they fuse, thus creating a lattice around the host tree's trunk. Gradually, they starve the host tree and prevent it from growing by robbing all its light, water, and nutrients. Eventually the banyan tree chokes the host until it dies and rots away, leaving the strangler fig standing in its place.'

This is where freedom started for me, and the reversal of years of damage. I was that tree and had the life of God sucked out of me. The realization came years later after learning what effects porn was having on me.

ONLY ONE ANSWER

'Our soul has escaped as a bird from the snare of the fowlers. The snare is broken, and we have escaped'. Psalm 124:7

A fowler is a professional bird catcher. In the days before firearms, birds were captured with nets spread on the ground. David said in Psalm 91:3, "Surely He shall deliver you from the snare of the fowler, and from the perilous pestilence." It is what happened to my soul. Jesus set me free and my journey into this wonderful life began with gusto.

I was forgiven of my sins and Jesus became my Savior. A new beginning in life was just handed to me and I was extremely excited about my newfound faith. After work, I handed out tracts to people who passed me by on the sidewalk. Those tracts were of the yellow bubble with two black eyes and a thin smile on its face. The caption read "Smile; Jesus loves you!" It was rush hour, and I smiled and told them that Jesus loved them. I received some frowns, but it was the smiles that made it all worthwhile.

In thinking of my newfound freedom, I concluded that I had escaped from the mindset that kept me locked up in despair and loneliness. The baggage I dragged about became lighter because somebody was helping me. I was so happy that I finally met God and He was going to deal with all my issues (Psalms 138:8).

Learning the ropes of Christianity is no cake walk, as I found out as the years passed. There were many growing pains, and doubtless there were more to come. But anyone knows that restoration requires time and patience from all parties to accomplish that work. When I say all parties, I'm referring to the individual, his or her friends, and God. Relationships are important in the ongoing struggle against sin.

John 3:16 declares the love of God in Jesus's own words: "God so loved the world that He gave His only Son, that whosoever believes in Him will not perish but have everlasting life." This is one of the most quoted scriptures of all time because of its truth and the hope it engenders in those souls who hear it and receive the truth of its meaning. If you were to substitute for the word 'world' with your name and read it that way, this portion of God's Word would be more personal to you.

There are other words that could be used besides the word 'believe' in John 3:16. The word believe means to trust in. the word 'perish' (as in perishable), means to die. Lost is a good description of where I was, and I believe that while I may have been looking for God, He is the one who found me. The hunter was ready to scoop me up in his net, but the Lord (Savior) held the net open and I was able to escape into the arms of my deliverer, Jesus Christ.

Being saved, or born again, is a central belief that's been around since Jesus's day. This truth means different things to different people. I like that Paul the apostle mentions that salvation is an ongoing process. The book of Romans says that we were saved when we accepted Jesus as our own personal Lord and Savior, we are being saved presently, and that we will be saved in the future. This process means maturity as we become more like Jesus. It also means that God is going to work on our hang-ups, our thinking, and our perceptions. Our battered souls will undergo a living transformation if we allow Him to do the work. David, in Psalm 23, says, "He leads me down the path of righteousness for His name's sake."

We see here that it's not all about us. And yes, while it is about us to choose God, if we do, we will begin to live lives that progressively are not all about us. The Lord wants us to live lives separate from the world and our old habits. That is why if we allow Jesus to lead us, He'll take us down the right path.

Are you experiencing confirmation bias in considering your attitude and worldview in sexual freedom? A confirmation bias is a type of cognitive bias that involves favoring information that confirms your previously existing beliefs or prejudices or to justify certain behaviours.

Psalms 10: 11–13 says that some believe that God is like them or is okay with their habits because he is silent with what they do.

Hear what it is that Jesus taught us about the parable of the sower.

"Therefore hear the parable of the Sower... now he who received seed among the thorns is he who hears the word, and the cares of this world and the deceitfulness of riches choke the word, and he becomes unfruitful. But he who received seed on the good ground is he who hears the word and understands it. It is he who indeed bears fruit and produces: some a hundredfold, some sixty, some thirty." (Mt 13:18, 22–23)

The word choke means to stifle (by drowning or overgrowth). I find the story above chilling as it applies to Christians who live lives full of compromise. Let's say that we replace the cares of this world with the words sexual impurity. This does bring it closer to home. Choking out the love of God from our lives does happen every time we practice sin.

Becoming unfruitful is a key word. We can say we've been sidelined, taken out of the game because we've allowed sexual impurity to fill the space where the Holy Spirit ought to dwell. The Bible states that we are the temple of the Holy Spirit. As James says, out of the well there should not come good drinking water and impure water at the same time (James 3:11).

There's also a story of King David praying to the Lord about his enemies, who were threatening the Land of Israel.

And David inquired of God, saying, "Shall I go up against the Philistines? Will You deliver them into my hand?" The LORD said to him, "Go up, for

I will deliver them into your hand." So they went up to Baal Perazim, and David defeated them there. Then David said, "God has broken through my enemies by my hand like a breakthrough of water." Therefore, they called the name of that place Baal Perazim. And when they left their gods there, David gave a commandment, and they were burned with fire. (1 Chronicles 14:10–12)

The words Baal Perazim in Hebrew translate as "master of breakthroughs." It was not only God's desire to give David victory but to lead him to destroy the remnants, or gods, that the Philistines had left behind.

When you have victory in a certain area, it is important to let go of those things that trip you up or are triggers in your recovery process.

I have always liked watching television. Four years ago, I became convicted regarding the number of hours I sat there like a dummy, wasting time. It also occurred to me that as I flipped through the channels, I ended watching something that I would call ungodly. This became a trigger to me. I prayed about it and the result was to give it up. In March 2017, I disconnected the cable.

This was not an easy decision, but looking back, it was the right decision. I did not do this on my own. I discussed this issue at length with my wife, and she agreed that the television was not an essential need.

I could almost hear Jesus say, "If your eye offends you, pluck it out." Today we would say, "If you can't control your television watching, then get rid of the television." This is one example of coming clean and marching toward victory.

Only Jesus can give us the kind of breakthrough that will really allow us to experience progressive victory over any addiction.

Soon after I accepted Jesus as Savior, I had a slip and was filled with lust. I masturbated. I remember the shame, and how much I wanted to be free. I found my Bible and flipped it open. My eyes landed on Psalms 138. I read the scriptures and verse 8 came to my attention. It said, "The Lord will perfect that which concerns me; your mercy, O Lord, endures forever; Do not forsake the works of your hands." Years later, I studied the meaning of that scripture. I found the word perfect to mean complete, to bring to an end, to cause to cease, or to eradicate that which the psalmist struggled with. I embraced the promise and moved on in my journey with the Lord. The idea that God was going to do this for me sent my hope meter sky high.

Here are some other biblical passages for your consideration.

- Psalms 14:2–3:
  "The LORD looks down from heaven upon the children of men,
  To see if there are any who understand, who seek God.
  They have all turned aside,

They have together become corrupt;

There is none who does good,

No, not one."

- Psalms 12:5–7 talks about the process for purification that the Lord has set out in His word.

- Psalms 23:3: "He leads me in the paths of righteousness for His name's sake."

JESUS HEALS TODAY

Please bear with me as we consider a few more portions of scripture and then I'm done.

Now it happened, as Jesus sat at the table in the house that behold, many tax collectors and sinners came and sat down with Him and His disciples. And when the Pharisees saw it, they said to His disciples, "Why does your teacher eat with tax collectors and sinners?" When Jesus heard that, He said to them, "Those who are well have no need of a physician, but those who are sick. But go and learn what this means: 'I desire mercy and not sacrifice.' For I did not come to call the righteous, but sinners, to repentance." (Matthew 9:10–15)

Jesus said to his disciples that it was not those who were well who needed a physician but those who were sick. I was a sick man. And I did not know it.

I knew something was not right, something not lined up properly—a warped habit, if you will allow, in many aspects in my life. It was not until I saw my poverty that I was willing to consider something beyond myself. It took hitting rock bottom to recognizing my addiction before I began to look for change in my life. When everything is going well, it is easy to ignore the real issues, because they're not fun.

When there's money in the bank, you have a

nice wife, and good children, everything is okay. What I did not know was occasionally glancing at porn, reading a Playboy magazine, and looking at young bikini models lustfully was not normal. The first glance is a curiosity thing but if it lingers, that's when the sinning starts.

Some say, come on, everybody does that, even Christians. Sadly, you are correct. I recently heard it quoted that 68% of Christians[8], both men and women, have issues with sexual eccentricities. While it is true that our culture is saturated with sex, to be always lustful is not the way God intended for us to live. In the world we live, this is passed off as normal behavior. It's our genetic make-up, they say. It is true to be attracted to the opposite sex is a normal part of growing up.

To allow lust to have sway in our bodies is the cause of so much heartache in our personal lives. It is not normal conduct to believe we can have

---

[8] 2016 Barna Research,,Culture & Media

whatever we want. It's not biblical behavior. What we do in the privacy of our homes does not reduce the seriousness of our actions. The Bible talks a lot about lust and how it leads down the slippery slope of increasingly sinful acts. It also causes us to disregard God's counsel to us. He deserves better than this.

If you study the life of Jesus, you cannot see that he lusted for anything, even when he was on the point of dying from thirst. The devil tempted him, but he saw right through that and never compromised. No wonder I needed a Savior; I spent way too many hours lusting for what I could not have.

I may have an addictive personality, and I'm not sure if that's a real thing. It may just be another convenient excuse. The problem with porn is that it's a portal to sin—and sin is never satisfied. We love God but cheat on Him. We love our wives but connect online with strangers. In retrospect, I find it bizarre that it was how I behaved at times.

A fact remains that those who do not know the Lord may endorse a lifestyle in which pornography use is viewed as normal. Others also slip into other vile practices as participants in an ungodly world. I'm talking about non-believers who do not know better.

There are some non-believers who put us to shame in terms of their lifestyle. We who are called by the name of the Lord had need to wake up to that reality. Paul the apostle says that these things or behaviors should not even be named among the believers. Consider what James says here: "Adulterers and adulteresses! Do you not know that friendship with the world is enmity with God? Whoever therefore wants to be a friend of the world makes himself an enemy of God" (James 4:4–6).

Many of us have brought our unregenerate lifestyles or pasts into our walks with God, and the Holy Spirit wants to clean house. To say in today's vernacular, this is where the rubber hits the road.

In the Old Testament, God promises healing: "If you diligently heed the voice of the LORD your God and do what is right in His sight, give ear to His commandments and keep all His statutes, I will put none of the diseases on you which I have brought on the Egyptians. For I am the LORD who heals you" (Exodus 15:26).

When I got to the point when I really wanted change, God was there ready to help me. He was able to do with me what I could not possibly do on my own in a lifetime. Thankfully He is patient with us. What do you want today? Is it peace of mind? Is it hope for tomorrow? Then you must close the door to porn. You cannot have it both ways.

The journey is only beginning when we finally understand that we are sinners, and that Jesus came to set us sinners free. There always must be a beginning to everything, and this applies to our born-again experience. This walk is not one that we can do alone, nor should we. Jesus died to set us free so that we can start moving in the direction that he has planned out for us.

In 2 Timothy 1:9–10, it says that it is God "who has saved us and called us with a holy calling, not according to our works, but according to His own purpose and grace which was given to us in Christ Jesus before time began, but has now been revealed by the appearing of our Savior Jesus Christ."

If you hung in there with me as you read this book, I thank you. I hope that if you are one of those guys who have benefitted from reading my story, then you will give thanks to the Lord. It was the Lord who impressed upon me to write my story.

Before we started this pilgrimage to the Promised Land, we had no idea about God's sovereignty. It is His uncanny ability to speak into our consciences, to let us know when we are veering off the track. And it is always at that point that we decide if we are going to listen and stop selling ourselves short, or keep doing the same old thing repeatedly with the same old results. You know that the definition of insanity is doing the same thing over again and expecting different results.

Jesus said come learn of me, for my burden is light and my yoke is easy (Matthew 11:30). He is inviting us to observe how to walk in unity with God, to experience peace during turmoil. We want to be successful in the daily grind of life and not lose it.

You're not expected to learn patience on the first day, but begin to learn it in small increments every day for the rest of your life. As a pastor said, we walk this walk one step at a time.

CONCLUSION

After eighteen years of praying and then talking to my doctor and pastor about the curvature of my penis, I came to a decision. It seems to me that the Lord said that this was done at my hands, and I must seek a solution at the hands of a specialist. I sought out the advice of a neurologist who told me that, while this kind of surgery was risky, it would be worth it.

In 1992, I underwent specialized surgery to repair the torn muscles of my sex organ. This had a positive effect on me. Over the next few years, I began to have a better self image. I grew more confident. My sex life with my wife improved. It got better because

I was more relaxed, more confident, and I listened to my wife better. Our biggest sex organ is in our brain. How we view and perceive ourselves with regards to our sexuality is of paramount importance.

I remember going through a period of grief about my history. I grieved the missed years of normal social activities all throughout my teenage years. I was surprised when I went through this. But it was necessary for me to experience this unique feeling of loss.

Healing is a part of God's overhaul of the Christian life. It's healing from past hurts and abuses, healing from failures, healing from other people failing us, healing from addictions, and healing from bad attitudes. The list goes on. We need healing, period, or Jesus would not have mentioned it and he would not have healed so many.

For healing to be effective in my life, I had to put it all on the line. It is my honest opinion that God is looking for those who not only need healing but for those who are genuine about getting it. Until that happens, compromises of personal values will continue. How do I know this? I lived a half-hearted commitment to personal purity for many years.

The other very important aspect of our personal healing is to confess our sins and to forgive others. It was very difficult for me to forgive certain people in my past. But I knew that to not do so would hamper the healing process in my life that the Lord had begun in me.

There are many good books on what healing does to help the addict overcome. I recommend that you ask Jesus in prayer, and listen to what He says to you about your situation right there and then. Be silent for a few minutes to hear the voice of the Spirit.

If you are still unsure whether God considers purity in our daily activities, please read portions of the book of Proverbs as listed below.

I was open with my past personal struggles.

I pray my openness has helped you to start the conversation in your own life. Take the necessary steps to find true peace with Christ.

And everyone who has this hope in Him purifies himself, just as He is pure. I John 3:3

What do you want today? Is it peace with God or just one more click of the mouse? You cannot have it both ways. Thankfully He is patient with us.

End

The Peril of Adultery

Proverbs 5:1–23

My son, pay attention to my wisdom;

Lend your ear to my understanding,

That you may preserve discretion,

And your lips may keep knowledge.

For the lips of an immoral woman drip honey,

And her mouth is smoother than oil;

But in the end she is bitter as wormwood,

Sharp as a two-edged sword.

Her feet go down to death,

Her steps lay hold of hell.

Lest you ponder her path of life—

Her ways are unstable;

You do not know them.

Therefore hear me now, my children,

And do not depart from the words of my mouth.

Remove your way far from her,

And do not go near the door of her house,

Lest you give your honor to others,

And your years to the cruel one;

Lest aliens be filled with your wealth,

And your labors go to the house of a foreigner;

And you mourn at last,

When your flesh and your body are consumed,

And say:

"How I have hated instruction,

And my heart despised correction!

I have not obeyed the voice of my teachers,

Nor inclined my ear to those who instructed me!

I was on the verge of total ruin,

In the midst of the assembly and congregation."

Drink water from your own cistern,

And running water from your own well.

Should your fountains be dispersed abroad,

Streams of water in the streets?

Let them be only your own,

And not for strangers with you.

Let your fountain be blessed,

And rejoice with the wife of your youth.

As a loving deer and a graceful doe,

Let her breasts satisfy you at all times;

And always be enraptured with her love.

For why should you, my son, be enraptured by an immoral woman,

And be embraced in the arms of a seductress?

For the ways of man are before the eyes of the LORD,

And He ponders all his paths.

His own iniquities entrap the wicked man,

And he is caught in the cords of his sin.

He shall die for lack of instruction,

And in the greatness of his folly he shall go astray.

Proverbs 6:20–35

My son, keep your father's command,

And do not forsake the law of your mother.

Bind them continually upon your heart;

Tie them around your neck.

When you roam, they will lead you;

When you sleep, they will keep you;

And when you awake, they will speak with you.

For the commandment is a lamp,

And the law a light;

Reproofs of instruction are the way of life,

To keep you from the evil woman,

From the flattering tongue of a seductress.

Do not lust after her beauty in your heart,

Nor let her allure you with her eyelids.

For by means of a harlot

A man is reduced to a crust of bread;

And an adulteress will prey upon his precious life.

Can a man take fire to his bosom,

And his clothes not be burned?

Can one walk on hot coals,

And his feet not be seared?

So is he who goes in to his neighbor's wife;

Whoever touches her shall not be innocent.

People do not despise a thief

If he steals to satisfy himself when he is starving.

Yet when he is found, he must restore sevenfold;

He may have to give up all the substance of his house.

Whoever commits adultery with a woman lacks understanding;

He who does so destroys his own soul.

Wounds and dishonor he will get,

And his reproach will not be wiped away.

For jealousy is a husband's fury;

Therefore he will not spare in the day of vengeance.

He will accept no recompense,

Nor will he be appeased though you give many gifts

Printed in the United States
by Baker & Taylor Publisher Services